# BRADFORD IN FOCUS

photographs by Tim Smith • introduction by Martin Wainwright

First published in 2003 by
Tim Smith Photos

ISBN 0-9546424-0-6

Editorial assistant: Elizabeth Smith
Production Assistant: Matt Doyle
Design: Raw Design UK Ltd
Printing: Wheelden Print Ltd

# CONTENTS

LISTER SPECIALS
KEBADER
MASALA FISH
SEEKH KEBAB
CHICKEN DONNER
ON FRESH NAAN

This book is dedicated to Isabelle Guillou,
who loved Bradford and who helped to make it a special place.

Bradford's bid to become the European Capital of Culture in 2008 was the spur for the production of this book. The photographs on the cover, and which introduce each section, were commissioned as part of the 2008 campaign, *One Landscape, Many Views*. Over 500 people living or working in the Bradford District were photographed, and the results were used to make up these mosaic pictures.

The bid was built on the views and aspirations of Bradford's people, and was successful in renewing a sense of purpose for Bradford's future. This book is intended to reflect the aims of the 2008 bid, and celebrates the strengths of the communities of the Bradford District and the places in which they live. It uses photographs taken over the past twenty years together with newly commissioned work taken especially for this book.

# ACKNOWLEDGEMENTS

It was the work of the 2008 team that turned the idea of this book into a reality, and special thanks are due to Anita Morris, Paul Brookes, Steve Manthorp and Emma Cheshire.

The production was made possible with the generous sponsorship of the Yorkshire Building Society. I would like to thank the company for their support, and Joanne Howarth and Tanya Mills for their personal involvement in the project.

I would also like to thank the following people:

My family, Elizabeth and Alexei, who are my love and inspiration.

The team at Elmwood who worked on the campaign for the 2008 bid, and produced the mosaic pictures.

For commissioning many of the pictures that are included here: Allan Brack and the team at Bradford Festival Ltd; Jill Kirkaldy at Bradford Education; Claire Ackroyd and colleagues at Bradford Art Galleries and Museums; the staff of the Marketing Department and Press Office at Bradford M.D.C.; staff on the picture desks of *The Guardian, Observer, Independent, The Times* and the *Times Educational Supplement*.

My deepest thanks go to all the people I have photographed, many of whom are not included here, and to those who have helped me along the way by taking me into their homes, their places of work, worship and recreation, and who have shared meals and conversations.

Tim Smith

The culture of the Bradford district is not just demonstrated by its buildings, galleries and museums, but the whole spectrum of life in the city. It's the people of Bradford that make it a vibrant and contemporary district, and all this is captured in this book.

Bradford's textile roots provided affluence and wonderful architecture, and have helped shape the city we enjoy today. Local businesses have always played an important role in the development of the Bradford community - Titus Salt and his philanthropic approach in Saltaire pioneered the integration of business in the Bradford community, which has continued for more than a century.

Today Bradford is a rich tapestry blending old and new. Traditional industries have been largely replaced with the focus on different areas including financial services, highly regarded educational institutions and even renowned sporting teams. The environment for people who live and work here can be fast moving, constantly adapting to the area's social and economic needs.

This book demonstrates that Bradford has something to offer everyone - from the picturesque and dramatic countryside on Ilkley Moor to the theatres and many festivals in the city, and we hope that it will help many more people appreciate the culture, diversity and beauty of our district.

Iain Cornish
Chief Executive,
Yorkshire Building Society

introduction by Martin Wainwright

Opposite Page: Bradford's very own Angel of the North was created by *Mind the Gap* theatre company. This strolling player was designed to stimulate debate about the role of the arts in the regeneration of the city, and is seen here outside Manningham Mills.

Above: A sculpture by Ian Randall welcomes arrivals at Forster Square station.

**When I first came to work in Bradford, there was a billboard outside the Baptist chapel in Wakefield Road announcing 'a warm welcome for our new minister, formerly of Ryde on the Isle of Wight'. I felt a surge of sympathy for this fellow-newcomer, who had so lately been looking out over the soft landscape of Hampshire and his pretty resort's ferry pier. I too was fresh from prettiness, the gentle countryside of Bath and north Somerset, and now we were both having to get used to a landscape of industry and stone.**

The minister had the advantage because he would have been familiar with the Biblical phrase about lifting up your eyes unto the hills from whence cometh mine help, something which took me a little longer. But within my first week, crossing Hall Ings or exploring Manningham Lane, I did glance up. I saw and enjoyed the usual plump cherubs and symbols of prosperity and thrift with which the Victorians decorated their commercial buildings. But then suddenly I was back in Bath.

Through the avenues of stone like Market Street and Kirkgate, whose original honey-colour and darker patina from age are shared by both cities, wedges of green hillside appeared invitingly in the distance. Instead of Sham Castle or Lansdown Folly, two of the belvederes of Bath, there were the quarry cliffs of Bolton Moor and the long green fields running up to the Brontë sisters' birthplace in Thornton. Beyond, and this is

something which the modest hills round Bath could not boast, were the purple edges of the Pennines and Ilkley Moor, the latter above the groves of Lister Park and its noisy, open-air, alas-vanished Lido which sent helpful splashes of water into the botanical garden next door.

All this was wonderful to explore, by bus and on foot, even occasionally by bicycle although Bradford's hills, which create the magnificent setting, are not kind to pedal power. My uncle, a long-serving local vicar who once lived in the Emmerdale TV soap opera rectory in the sewage-workers' hamlet of Esholt, told me a story about this. An acquaintance of his father's, a textile magnate wanting to save petrol in wartime (and wanting people to know about his good deed) bought six bicycles and freewheeled into the city centre every morning. Then - the return journey to Heaton being impossibly steep - one of his firm's lorries brought the whole lot back at the weekend. He must have trammed it in the evening, or even gone home by horse.

Horses. Who would expect them to be grazing placidly in the city of muck and brass? But there they are, one of the first unexpected treasures I discovered on my early wanderings through a landscape more subtle and surprising than the expensive and manicured surroundings of Bath. There seemed to be hardly a patch of green which wasn't being used as a corral, with ponies and the occasional bigger, racehorse-like animal tethered Apache-style within yards of the rush-hour traffic. Go and have a look. They're still there. Later I got to know Terry Singh, Bradford Council's animal welfare officer, who introduced me to many other species which share the city with

its resident humans. A veteran of heroic round-ups which would have delighted Wyatt Earp or Buffalo Bill (he once chased escaped horses four abreast up the dual carriageway of Manchester Road), he explained the city's place as a staging post on the horse-trading route to Appleby Fair. I also learned about the long-distance footpaths of urban foxes, and the complicated twice-daily commute of the starlings which whirl over Bradford's Victorian crenellations at dusk.

It was all unexpectedly green and pleasant and it remains so, as Tim's photographs reveal. That is the first attraction of Bradford for me. But it is bound up with the second. We don't have a chocolate box sort of scenery. It is a greenery criss-crossed with human traces and moulded by human interference; vibrant with the evidence of busy people inventing money-making things to do. The trolley bus made its debut here, along with mail order (all honour to the former Italian pedlar Enrico Fattorini who created Grattan's). The writer J.B. Priestley's father invented the school meals system at his Manningham primary. Soon afterwards, councillors installed the country's first school swimming pool. It all came together for me when I did a piece for *The Guardian* on a new mountain bike called the 'Bradford' which had been patented by the University of Bradford. We needed an appropriate backdrop for a photograph and I found myself puffing through allotments, ginnels and wasteland to some terraces overlooking Bradford City's football ground at Valley Parade.

Top Right: Church in Little Horton, Bradford.
Above: The Worth Valley.

The wide panorama from here had stupendous grandeur, decorated with swathes of greenery in the street trees and the tangle of buddleia and willowherb around us. Like other Northern cities, Bradford becomes wonderfully softer and more enticing in the summer, stretching into the autumn when you can pick blackberries within sight of the transport interchange. But the 'bicycle view' was also made up of a maze of interesting constructions and people using the steep slope right down to the Bradford Beck. Busy, busy, busy. So it has been since the first town fathers built the Broad Ford over a stream whose rapid and clean water was perfect for their way of making a living - wool.

That stream is now a prisoner of Bradford. I wish its cell could be broken open and lined with weeping willows, much as the council has made such excellent, well-planted use of the old Exchange station wall, sweeping round from Petergate to Hall Ings. I entered Bradford Beck's dark world once for a feature on Victorian sewerage, slipping down a manhole in front of City Hall and wading through the mighty brick-lined culvert way beyond Forster Square. The tunnel is matched only by another secret of the city waiting modestly to be discovered: the titanic outfall from the city to Esholt sewage works, my reverend uncle's old domain. So big is this, that it was opened with a drive-through by a fleet of locally-made Jowett cars led by the Lord Mayor. When they emerged at the Esholt end (a Dante-esque portal which you can still see from the Leeds-Liverpool Canal towpath), the architect's wife is supposed to have muttered - smarting from a dispute over fees perhaps: 'Here comes the first load of shit'.

Sloshing along the subterranean Bradford Beck risks occasional murky encounters with things in the water whose nature is best not investigated. But this provides one of the best metaphors coined to describe my third reason for delighting in Bradford: the almost unparalleled richness of the human landscape. As I settled in to my first home in Southfield Square in Manningham, I could spend a day something like this. Early morning stroll with a Latvian woolcomber, buy papers from a Pakistani born close

to the Khyber Pass; breakfast with Nancy and Karl Boychuk the irrepressible Ukrainians - Nancy so like a Matrioshka doll that it was hard not to tap her to hear the rattle of six or seven smaller Nancies inside. Then work, alongside several Scots and a Trinidadian, lunch at a Bangladeshi curry house and a job in the afternoon researching a feature on the different Christmas arrangements of the Serbian Orthodox community. On from there to the Estonian Club and a chat with its elegant, silver-haired secretary; and finally tea with some more Estonians, my

neighbours Karin and Alex Parbus, formerly of Talinn, whose daughter Maggie had played as a child in Southfield Square with one of my teenage pin-ups, the Bradford-born film star Mary Tamm.

They have left me with one of my most moving images of Bradford's diversity: a gentle, flickering light illuminating several very different faces, a bearded Sikh's, an Anglo-Indian woman's soft rounded features, and the high cheekbones of several

View from Southfield Square along Carlisle Place, Manningham.

Statue of J.B. Priestley overlooking City Hall.

Slavs. The light came from the candles which the Parbuses lit on their Christmas tree. An enthralling alternative to fairy lights, even if buckets of water had to be handily by.

Bradford's gutsy bid to be European Capital of Culture built on this extraordinary human tapestry with its slogan *One Landscape Many Views*. But it was Priestley who got there first with his comparison of this cultural mixture to the Bradford beck. J.B. Priestley stands above the hidden watercourse today, massive and with his stout overcoat (a Bradford sartorial essential) forming wings behind him, outside the front of the National Museum of Film, Photography and Television. But picture him as a lad in the offices of local mills, before he took the train to London and started getting his stories of 'Bruddersford' into print.

He overheard the guttural expressions of Germans, textile entrepreneurs from Bremen and Hamburg who settled here, among them the Delius family whose son is now ranked among the greatest 'English' composers. Priestley listened to the quickfire banter of Yiddish. He heard masses of scarcely-comprehensible Scots. Then he thought about the beck running darkly in its culvert below, and the stretches out towards Shipley where dumped dye waste (a very expensive environmental crime nowadays) turned the water peacock colours. And so he wrote of the 'incomers' adding an exotic dash of grand Continental rivers like the Rhine and the Oder to 'our grim runnel - t'mucky beck' and added '..it is not that these German Jews were better men than we are. The point is that they were different. They acted as a leaven, just as a colony of typical West Riding folk would act as a leaven in Munich or Moscow'.

Include among them Fattorini the Italian, W.E. Forster the creator of state education who came from Dorset to set up a woolstapling business. Don't forget Milligan the first city mayor, a thoroughgoing Borders Scot. Or Norman Angell, the Nobel Peace Prize winner and MP for Bradford North who came here from Lincolnshire via California. That is the spirit in which Bradford is dealing today with the much larger leaven of late 20th century newcomers, often described en masse as 'Asians' but much more fruitful to dissect into all their marvellous and very different cultures - Pakistani, Bangladeshi, Indian and many more. Like the German textile men, like the European Voluntary Workers who were sent to Bradford in 1946 (nothing voluntary; they included refugees and 'enemy aliens' and they were forced to go wherever workers were needed), the latest Bradfordians are a huge source of energy. I remember going on the coat-tails of Lady Thatcher round one of the many British Asian-run businesses which have sprung up in the city, adding to local wealth and creating jobs. Their product was a range of utterly Yorkshire bakery lines - breadcakes, barm-cakes, pikelets - all sold under some marvellous ethnic label (ethnic Yorkshire that is) on the lines of Old Mother Heckinbotham's Farm Produce.

View across the Thornton Road area towards Manningham Mills.

Food is my fourth anchor to Bradford, and satisfyingly it forms one of the most distinct links between those successive generations of enterprising immigrants. Famously, there are few better places in Europe to find a curry, and it is worth seeking out the modest dives where you don't use cutlery - chapatis are much easier and add variety to the taste of every mouthful. There was a glorious - at last they've got the point - moment in 2003 when the very Southern, metropolitan design magazine *Blueprint* featured a huge picture of one of the most divey curry dives in Bradford on its front cover. It was an occasion matched in my experience only by the amazing appearance of Cartwright Hall's formal bedding gardens as the cover illustration of pearl- and mansion-strewn *Country Life* magazine in the early 1990s.

The quality of cuisine today would have been appreciated by earlier incomers - for example, the Delius family and their fellow Germans. I remember being kindly invited to that curious survival the Bradford Club, tucked away in an alley among all

Mill in the Worth Valley, now used by engineering firm Airedale Springs.

the grand city centre banks, and there shown the minute book for the first years of the 20th century. It recorded the growing frustration of German members with the dismal quality of English cooking and, in the end, a revolution which saw the Germans take over at the stove, to the eventual satisfaction of all. Because, lapping up their friends' goulash or sauerkraut, Bradford businessmen were as cosmopolitan then as they are now. A textile magnate would know the rail and shipping connections across the world as a result of his pursuit of fibres to spin, just as today a Bradford Bulls scout will have an encyclopaedic knowledge of the best young rugby players Down Under.

But then and now, these citizens of the world have been strangely reluctant to show off their knowledge. They are frightened of being guyed, maybe, or considered as people putting on airs. At all events, there has grown up a Bradford mannerism of disguise. People who are immensely learned and entertaining in private take on a public persona of provincial ignorance. They willingly adopt the misleading part which T.S. Eliot snobbishly wrote for them in his lines about '..one of the low on whom assurance sits, as a silk hat on a Bradford millionaire'.

Modesty about real virtues can be an attractive personal characteristic, but it is damaging when taken to the extremes in which these Bradfordians seem to delight. It is time for some criticism. A mawkish strain which does not endear the city to me goes back to the old Civil War story about an angel appearing to the Duke of Newcastle, the Royalist commander, as he slept in Bolling Hall the night before he was to bombard the Parliamentarians' garrison. They were holed up in the parish church (now the Cathedral) which they had fortified with wool bales like sandbags. 'Pity poor Bradford!' beseeched the vision. The appeal worked. But unfortunately it has become almost a civic motto ever since.

Bradfordians' tendency to put their own city down has got dangerously close to being a self-fulfilling prophecy in modern times. It didn't matter when the place was superheated economically, when locals were so ingenious and productive that they even made soap and lipstick from Esholt's sewage, which was oily with lanolin from the wool-washing drains of the local mills. But when hard times come for tops and noils, and when the vigour of the ethnic communities boils over into frustration and the Manningham street battles, a constant tendency to be glum is unhelpful indeed.

It reached a climax when the Capital of Culture bid, playing on Bradfordians' cynicism, employed the slogan 'Oh Ye of Little Faith' in its attempts to get citizens excited about something other than Gareth Gates. It is also exacerbated by the nearby hype and fireworks constantly thrown up by Big Neighbour Leeds. The psychology there is exactly the opposite, a place which for ever talks itself up. That is a medicine which Bradford needs to take.

But another remedy has been masterfully encouraged by the city, ever since a brass band, the Lord Mayor and a red carpet greeted a startled pensioner from Sussex, Ted Adams, at the railway station as 'Bradford's first tourist' on 22 October 1980. There are now millions of tourists every year, and their immersion in the reality of the city is the best answer to

carping. They are lost for a whole day in the wonders of the National Museum of Film, Photography and Television. They shop 'till they drop in Bombay Stores. They might even see Gareth Gates or his successor Kimberley Walsh from Allerton (always pronounced 'Ollerton' just as Bradford, to a Bradfordian, is 'Bratford'). Or Linda Barker, the svelte queen of the house and garden TV makeover, whose roots are in the Girls' Grammar School and her parents' home in Shelf.

There is another unit of the US Cavalry riding to the rescue too. Bradford today is a much more extensive place than the old city was, when its borders stopped abruptly at Six Days Only in Heaton and All Alone Road above Idle. You are in Bradford now until you climb out of Addingham, cross the bridge at Kildwick and clamber breathlessly to the summit of Top Withens - Wuthering Heights - moor. The modern city includes the world-famous shrine of the Brontës in Haworth, whose signposts in Japanese are much-used by visitors. Extremely prosperous Ilkley also comes under its wing.

Some people in this beautiful and historic girdle do not like this arrangement and grumble about independence or the

Beware of those bearing gifts... Street entertainers emerge from their hiding place inside a Trojan Horse at the launch of the Bradford Festival.

Manufacture of medal ribbons at The Wyedean Weaving Company in Haworth.

advantages of an LS (for Leeds) rather than BD postcode. They need a dose of John F Kennedy. 'Ask not what Bradford can do for you (and actually it does do a great deal). Ask what you can do for Bradford'. If the outer areas work together with the core - and this is another feature of Leeds' success - the results are dynamic.

The great proof of this is the breathtaking phenomenon of Saltaire and the role played in its creation and restoration by three most untypical - or are they? - Bradford men. The vast alpaca mill (see opposite page) and its tight grid of 'model' houses built for Sir Titus Salt's workers, were a national sensation when they were opened. Gradually they became an unremarkable part of an accepted landscape. And then, with the sudden power of a champagne cork flying off, they became part of a global agenda. Knock me down with a flying shuttle - the place was made a World Heritage Site in December 2001.

That ranks Saltaire, as you will be told repeatedly when visit it, with Angkor Wat and the Pyramids. React how you like, that is UNESCO's view and it was the unwavering vision of the mill's restorer Jonathan Silver.  He deserved to be a Sir Jonathan as much as Salt was a worthy Sir Titus, but he died of cancer too soon. Yet his incredible energy and ability to enlist people, many a dour and pessimistic Bradfordian among them, did its work before his body gave out. Some of the people who have turned parts of Saltaire into an Airedale version of Hebden Bridge put it about that he was old Salt reincarnated. Certainly Jonathan and Titus will be finding much common ground in Heaven.

The last of the Saltaire trio is David Hockney, my final reason for loving this city and another paragon of what Bradford can produce and what Bradfordians should be. It is only a shame that he has chosen for most of his life to make his home somewhere warmer and therefore far away. But he comes back a lot and when he does, he turns the dull grey tones of the caricature city - the cobbles, rain, leafless trees and derelict mills so tediously used as stereotypes - into primary colours. His galleries in Salts Mill GLOW. They are luminous. He painted a wonderful stamp of the mill, all golden orange and sky blue.

He produced an unforgettable cover for the Bradford telephone directory, showing the famous hill-climbing trams whose window-lit shapes at night were compared, with Hockney-like bravura, to jewelled beetles by the great West Riding writer Phyllis Bentley. My only dilemma has been choosing for my gallery of Bradford heroes between Hockney and his brother Paul - an accountant and Liberal Lord Mayor of the city who wore Union Jack socks and, crucially in a place which has done so much for Britain's prosperity, looked after the artist's books.

Martin Wainwright
Northern Editor
*The Guardian*

# WORK

Bradford district owes much of its industrial development to a mixture of geography and geology. Both the raw materials and the sources of power to process them were present in the land. The raw materials were stone, coal and iron; the power was fast-flowing water and then steam engines fed by coal.

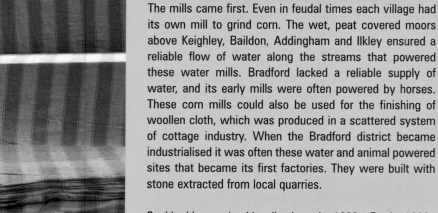

Above: Burling and mending at Drummond's.

Far Right: An old flywheel from the Low Moor Ironworks, one of the companies that made Bradford a major iron manufacturing centre in the nineteenth century.

A Jowett Jupiter high performance sports car built by Jowett Cars whose factory in Idle built up to 100 vehicles a week during the 1930s.

The mills came first. Even in feudal times each village had its own mill to grind corn. The wet, peat covered moors above Keighley, Baildon, Addingham and Ilkley ensured a reliable flow of water along the streams that powered these water mills. Bradford lacked a reliable supply of water, and its early mills were often powered by horses. These corn mills could also be used for the finishing of woollen cloth, which was produced in a scattered system of cottage industry. When the Bradford district became industrialised it was often these water and animal powered sites that became its first factories. They were built with stone extracted from local quarries.

Coal had been mined locally since the 1600s. By the 1800s hundreds of collieries were scattered throughout the area. The largest were concentrated in the coal basin of inner Bradford and run by companies such as the Bowling Iron Company and the Low Moor Company. As well as the coal ideal for feeding forges and furnaces, they extracted fireclays, metals and other minerals used to make iron and steel. The economic advantages of being able to mine all these materials together were huge, and as the companies expanded they exported their products all over the world via the Bradford Canal, which joined the Leeds-Liverpool Canal at Shipley. The cannons fired at the Battle of Trafalgar were made at Low Moor, and the Sydney Harbour Bridge is made from Low Moor Plate. These companies later went on to provide the metal for the manufacture of textile machinery.

Industrialisation of textiles followed in the wake of stone, iron and coal. Water was important not only for the generation of steam, but also for wool processing such as washing and dying, and as a means of flushing away industrial waste. This combination of natural resources and local enterprise was the foundation on which Bradford grew to become the woollen textiles capital of the world. Bradford's first textile mill opened in 1799. Fifty years later it had 129 mills and one third of the labour force of the UK worsted trade.

A huge range of other industries such as communications and financial services evolved to support textiles. The chemical industry supplied, among others, Ripley's Bowling Dyeworks, the largest textile dyeworks in the world. The printing industry produced literature in dozens of languages to promote Bradford products internationally. Keighley also made the machinery for mills in the area, and firms such as Prince-Smith and Stells (spinning frames), Hattersley's (looms) and Dean Smith and Grace (lathes) went on to supply to the textile and engineering industries worldwide.

By 1900 the number of mills in Bradford had grown to 350, but Bradford was no longer in a position of world dominance. The twentieth century saw firms such as Salts, Drummond's, Jeromes, and Foster's continue to produce worsteds in huge volumes. Lister's silks, velvets and knitting wools were sold internationally. The unique Conditioning House graded wool and cloth from all over the world, and traders at the Wool Exchange clinched multi-million pound deals by word alone, but the overall picture has been one of decline. Textiles came under

pressure from changes in fashion, from foreign competition and the erection of trade barriers overseas.

The Second World War marked a turning point. Textiles seemed to offer fewer job prospects than the emerging National Health Service or new firms like International Harvester's tractors, Grattan's mail-order and Baird Television where 5,000 people once made most of the country's TVs. A post-War demand for textiles enabled firms to modernise, and they recruited affordable labour from overseas. The respite was short-lived. Between 1961 and 1978 numbers working in textiles fell from nearly 73,000 to less than 28,000. Over the past twenty-five years the decline has been even more dramatic. The week before Christmas 2002 the closure of yet another local firm took the number of people working in textiles below 1,000. In the past 40 years 98% of the jobs have disappeared.

Wool is now processed by the countries that produce it, such as Australia, South Africa and Uruguay. Other production has gone to areas with lower labour costs, and as manufacturers closed locally, machinery has been sold

Above: A Keighley bolt and screw maker, Richard Hattersley started producing rollers, spindles and fliers in 1789, and eventually went on to produce looms sold all over the world. Many of them are still in use, such as this one used for weaving samples in Bradford.

Left: Disused yarn in a pattern weaving shop.

Below: The term worsted is used to describe yarns made from raw wool which has the short fibres removed by combing and the long fibres laid parallel to produce a smooth, even yarn. The yarn is the basic material from which knitted or woven fabric is made.

to places such as China and - most recently - Eastern Europe. Those firms that survive today have found a niche, often at the high quality end of the market. William Halstead's at Dudley Hill supplies cloth to Italian tailors making suits. Clissold's have a particularly strong marketing and design team based in central Bradford. Many of the wool trading fraternity are still operating here, old established firms who buy from producing countries and sell to processors.

Jobs have also declined in engineering, the other big sector of traditional manufacturing industry. Firms closely allied to the textile industry have disappeared or have developed new products to survive. Instead of looms and spinning frames engineers in Keighley now make lifts and escalators. Denso Marston in Shipley is

a leading manufacturer of car parts. Spooner Industries in Ilkley have adapted technology originally designed for the textile industry towards a range of new markets. Other industries with a long history in the area have evolved too. Ciba Speciality Chemicals have their largest factory in the world in Bradford, on the site at Low Moor that once made dyestuffs. Printing and packaging continue to be important, and Hallmark Cards have recently moved their UK headquarters to the district. Mail order is thriving, with Redcat (formerly Empire Stores) and Grattan remaining two of the biggest employers in the district. Wm Morrison Supermarkets, who opened their first supermarket in Bradford in 1961, are now one of the biggest food retailers in Britain and continue to grow in size. There have also been significant increases in employment in

banking and financial services, professional and scientific services, and public administration. Electronic engineering has become an important industry. Filtronic is a major supplier to the global mobile communications industry. Its close neighbour in Saltaire is Pace, which makes television receiving equipment.

Bradford has also made pioneering efforts in the field of tourism and the generation of leisure employment. The future may well lie in a mixture of the past and new developments, retaining a slimmed-down manufacturing base, with the continued development of service industries, a dash of high technology and a buoyant tourist and leisure industry. Together they may create the jobs and the environment where past and present mix for the benefit of Bradford and its people.

It took more than 50 years for all the processes involved in worsted production to be mechanised. Wool was combed and its fibres separated by hand right up until the 1840s when Samuel Cunliffe Lister developed a successful wool-combing machine. He made a fortune from his invention, and he used the money to build the biggest mill in Bradford, Lister's Manningham Mills. This statue in Lister Park commemorates him. Murals depicting the development of textiles from a cottage industry to factory production decorate the base of the statue. Ironically, the murals also show how reliant the industry was upon the labour of women and children.

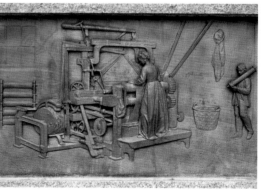

Opposite: Evidence of the once extensive coal industry can still be found, such as these spoil heaps next to old pit workings on Baildon Hill. Shallow pits and quarries were dug in upland areas, while shaft mining was used to extract coal from the valleys.

Extracting and cutting stone at the Hard York Quarries in Fagley. Quarrying was once a hugely important local industry, supplying stone to local builders and further afield. London was said to be paved with gold because of the colour of Yorkshire stone slabs produced in Bradford. Stone from the quarry shown here was used to construct local buildings such as Cartwright Hall; more recently, the quarry has produced stone for work on York Minster, Windsor Castle, and Buckingham Palace.

Opposite: Flagstones ready for sale at the Pickard Group's Bolton Woods quarry.

Water was the original source of power in the area, and most of the early textile mills can be found next to watercourses.

Clockwise from Top Left: Hewenden Mill on Hallas Beck near Cullingworth is now being converted into holiday flats.

A water wheel being reconstructed at Bradford Industrial Museum.

Griff's Mill on the River Worth near Stanbury has been derelict for many years.

Opposite: The Leeds-Liverpool Canal passing through Salts Mill at Saltaire. It was the incorporation of Keighley and Bradford into the national canal network that provided the cheap transport essential to the development of their industries. The Bradford Canal joined the Leeds-Liverpool at Shipley, but it was filled in after it fell into disuse with the coming of the railways.

The Clay family have been hill farmers in the Denholme area for over a century. They are seen here driving sheep over Oxenhope Moor towards more sheltered pastures for the winter. Sheep farming has always been important locally but could never satisfy the textile industry's demand for wool. Even in the days of cottage industry wool was imported from the East Riding, and by the time Bradford was known as 'Worstedopolis', wool was imported here from all over the world.

Manufacturing textiles at two of Bradford's best known firms, Drummond's and Lister's. Both firms closed during the 1990s. At its height Lister's provided jobs for over 5,000 people in its Manningham Mills alone, and as late as 1994 the Drummond Group employed 900 people, mainly at their Lumb Lane premises seen above.

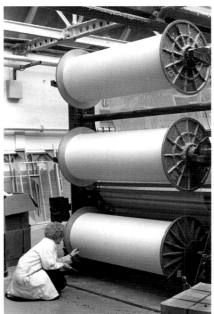

# WORK

Top: Punching out Jacquard pattern cards at Drummond's Lumb Lane Mills. It has been justifiably claimed that the loom was the first computer, in that it used a binary system to programme the machines, which could produce an infinite variety of patterns.

Bottom: Finishing department at Drummond's.

Above: An electrician working in the power generation room at Manningham Mills shortly before the mill was decommissioned.

Opposite Page: Empty weaving shed at Lister's Manningham Mills. Work began in 2003 on an ambitious scheme to transform the derelict site into a mixture of residential and business premises.

Above: Pattern weavers at Lumb Lane Mills producing samples for the Parkland Group. There were once hundreds of such highly skilled jobs; these men estimate that there are now less than twenty pattern weavers left in the area.

Right: Weaving department making material for J.H. Clissold and Son, who export menswear fabrics all over the world.

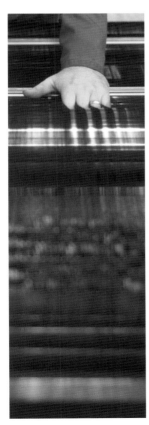

The products of the Wyedean Weaving Company in Haworth have been worn by everyone from the Queen to Michael Jackson, Idi Amin to Russell Crowe.

Wyedean's make braid and uniform accoutrements, and they produce an extraordinary range of woven and sewn materials used for an international range of medals, uniforms and costumes.

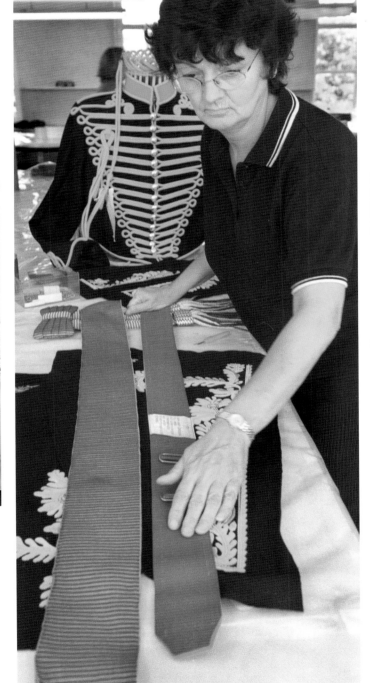

The bulk of Wyedean's work comes from making regalia for British state occasions and supplying armed forces all over the world. Designers such as Jean Paul Gaultier and film costumiers involved in movies from *Chitty Chitty Bang Bang* to the latest Hollywood blockbuster, *Hornblower*, provide them with more unusual challenges.

Leach and Thompson run one of the few traditional foundries left in Yorkshire, operating from a converted chapel in Keighley. Patterns carved from wood are used to shape the moulds, which are made from special sands.

When the moulds are ready, they are laid out in boxes on the floor of the foundry. The furnace is fuelled with coal, fed with scrap metal and limestone, and the resulting molten metal is then poured into the moulds to produce the castings. The final process is fettling, when the rough edges are abraded away.

Dean, Smith and Grace were a Keighley firm dating back to 1865 and were known internationally for the quality of their lathes. When the firm was acquired and then closed down by its new owners, former employees set up a new company, DSG Lathes. DSG continue to provide spares and service for the machines Dean, Smith and Grace built up to 50 years ago, as well as making a range of new lathes.

Spooner Industries are an Ilkley company founded in 1932 by William Wycliffe Spooner, who developed the industrial drying machine used for finishing fabrics. The firm have adapted this technology and now supply ovens, driers and coolers for a wide range of uses, including paper making, food manufacture and metal processing. The machinery being made in these pictures will go to a steel making plant in Canada.

WORK

Pace are a micro-electronics firm who make digital receiving equipment for televisions. Set up by a former engineer from Baird Television, they are based at Salts Mill where these pictures were taken. Their headquarters remain on this site, but they recently moved their manufacturing plant overseas to make use of lower labour costs.

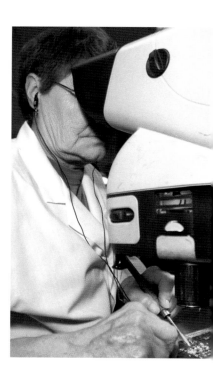

Opposite Page and Above Right: Filtronic are another electronic engineering firm based in Saltaire. Their products are widely used in the aerospace and mobile communications industries. Founded 25 years ago by David Rhodes, who worked from his bedroom and garage, Filtronic now have an annual turnover of around £300 million and employ thousands of people in the UK, USA, Finland, China and Australia.

The printing industry has been important in the district since it grew up to promote the products of other local industries, particularly textiles and engineering. Firms such as Fine Art Developments, Watmoughs and Lund Humphries have been major employers and a large percentage of the magazines and greetings cards sold around Britain are printed in Bradford.

Above: Many of the printing presses once used in the area were made in Wharfedale, and are now on display at Bradford Industrial Museum.

The most visible printing press in the city is the one that produces Bradford's local paper, the *Telegraph and Argus*. Many other local, regional and national titles have also been printed in the large glass press hall since it was built in 1981.

Above: Huge rolls of paper on the lower floor of the building feed the presses above.

Above: Feeding the paper through the machinery that will print, fold, collate and cut it to make a newspaper.

Top Right: Fixing the aluminium plates on to the rollers that will transfer the ink to the paper.

Right: Checking a finished copy for print quality.

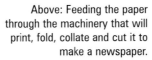

Coldspring Mill near Cullingworth was built in 1880 on the site of a natural soft water spring. This soap mill, an early example of a chemical factory, used lanolin from a nearby flay pit and tannery, where the hides of animals were flayed, stripped and cleaned before being made into leather belting to run mill machinery. The soap made at Coldspring Mill was used for scouring wool before the invention of detergents. For many years, this building was used for storing textile waste. It has now been renovated as a tearooms and shop selling outdoor clothing and equipment.

The site at Low Moor is Ciba Speciality Chemicals' biggest manufacturing plant in the world, with over 1,200 employees. Ciba make chemicals used in the production of paints, car parts, furnishing fabrics and paper. Their chemicals are also used for treating sewage, industrial effluents, and for the extraction of oil and minerals. The Low Moor site was originally the home of Allied Colloids, a firm established in 1935 to supply textile firms with chemicals for processing and dying wool and fabrics. Allied Colloids later diversified into chemicals for water treatment before Ciba acquired them in 1998.

The Yorkshire textile region became a centre for early building societies, which remain important today. The first building societies grew out of freehold land societies formed to enable working men to buy small plots of land and houses and thus be eligible to vote in local elections. Soon the societies' role in helping people to buy their own houses became more important, and the building societies grew rapidly. They also helped to raise the standard of building as it was in their interest to make sure that houses were of a suitable quality for investment.

Yorkshire Building Society is the third largest society in the UK and employs 1,200 people at its headquarters in Bradford. Its roots go back to the 1860s when the Huddersfield Equitable Permanent Benefit Building Society was formed. The Bradford Self Help Permanent Building Society, which later merged with the Huddersfield, was created in 1885. It was open to its 43 members in St. George's Hall Coffee Tavern once a week for just an hour and a half. The Huddersfield & Bradford and West Yorkshire Building Societies merged in 1982 and the Yorkshire Building Society was born.

Enrico Fattorini, the founder of Grattan, started in business selling jewellery made by the family firm from a shop in Bradford's Manchester Road. As business expanded catalogues were used to advertise products, and by the 1920s the company was retailing nationwide. The firm now dispatches 300,000 parcels a week from its computerised warehouse complex in Listerhills, Bradford.

Mrs Robinson has sold sweets from her shop on Northgate in Baildon for the past forty years.

Left: Morrisons, the family owned supermarket chain, was originally set up in 1899 as an egg and butter merchant in Bradford. The company went on to open its own market stalls and then shops with over the counter service. In the 1960s, Morrisons was at the forefront of supermarket development, opening its first self service store, "Victoria," in Bradford in 1961. Its flagship premises at Five Lanes End in Idle is built on the former site of International Harvesters, the tractor manufacturer.

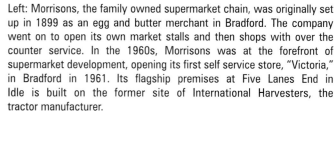

WORK

Above: The elaborate interior of the Wool Exchange. It was the capital of the wool trading world where men engaged in the combing, spinning, manufacturing, dyeing and selling of wool textile goods could meet and trade. It now houses a branch of Waterstones, the national bookshop chain.

Right: Shopping for sari lengths at an Indian Trade Mission show at Cartwright Hall in Bradford. There are hundreds of Asian fabric shops in the district and some of them, like Bombay Stores in Bradford, attract customers from all over the North.

The leisure and tourism industry is an increasingly important part of Bradford's economy, and people come from all over the world to visit the Brontë Parsonage at Haworth (Opposite Page). It was the home of the Brontë family between 1820 and 1861, and is where such books as *Wuthering Heights* and *Jane Eyre* were written.

This Page: These days, the Brontë name has strayed far from its literary origins to become a regional brand endorsing everything from taxis to frozen chickens.

Left: There is a vast range of places to eat in the area, including over 300 Asian restaurants.

The Box Tree Restaurant in Ilkley has a national reputation for its fine French cuisine. Its near neighbour Betty's Tearooms is equally well known as a source of traditional English food.

The National Health Service provides work for people in the area. The Bradford District has three major hospitals, St. Luke's Hospital, Bradford Royal Infirmary and Airedale Hospital.

Above and Right: Nurses at work on the medical wards at Bradford Royal Infirmary.

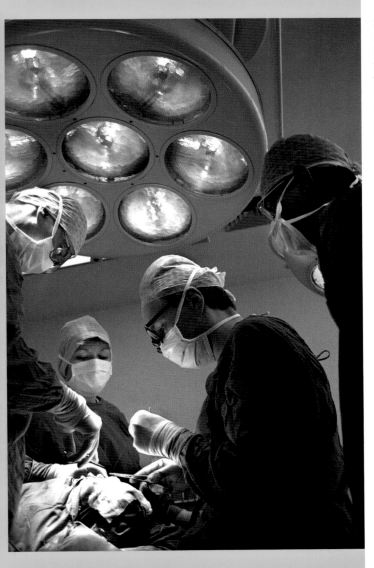

Surgeons carrying out
plastic surgery at
St. Luke's Hospital,
which is well known
for its pioneering work
in this field, much of it
developed in the wake
of the fire at the Valley
Parade football ground.

Idle Medical Centre,
Bradford.

Sandy Needham, Chief Executive of the Bradford Chamber of Commerce. This organisation offers a wide range of support and advice services to members. It has offices in Little Germany, which is also home to many other firms in the service industries, such as insurance companies and business consultancies.

John Pennington is a former President of the Bradford Chamber of Commerce. He is seen here in Pennington's, his variety club in Manningham, one of the biggest entertainment venues in West Yorkshire.

# LANDSCAPE

In its early days Bradford Dale would have been as quiet and picturesque as any of the valleys which now attract visitors to the Yorkshire Dales National Park. Small settlements in forest clearings would have clustered along the banks of the beck that ran through the valley. In the heart of the valley several tracks intersected and crossed the beck at the site known as Broad Ford. A regular traffic of people and goods led to the growth of a larger settlement here, which gradually developed into the commercial and administrative centre of the dale. Over time the settlement of 'Broad Ford' became Bradford.

Beef cattle near Clayton.

This needle sculpture on Cheapside vividly evokes Bradford's vanished textile industry.

Visitors who arrived in Bradford before the Industrial Revolution could remark upon its "verdant fields and fruitful gardens and purling trout streams". Keighley's first historian, the Reverend Miles Gale, wrote in1733 of a River Aire seething with dace, grayling, trout and salmon; and of abundant otters "which we suppose to feed on mussels, because the shells are generally found empty". But once the first mill arrived in the valley bottom the great bowl that is Bradford became the home of the power loom rather than the otter. Along the seemingly modest flow of the River Worth alone came Ponden Mill, Spring Head and Higher Providence, Dalton Mill, Low Mill, Walk Mill, East and West Greengate, Grove Mill, Damens Mill...

Since the first forest clearings this landscape has been defined by human industry. Canals, railways and roads were built along the valley bottoms to carry raw materials in and finished products out. As Bradford was transformed into the worsted capital of the world, its new found wealth found expression in opulent industrial and civic architecture inspired by the Italian Renaissance and built from local golden sandstone. Bradford claimed to have the "biggest silk mill" and the "longest mill frontage" in the world. The extraordinary Wool Exchange, for a century the centre of the world wool trade, demonstrated the riches and pride of the textile barons who mingled within it. In Keighley the Mechanic's Institute had a library, exhibition gallery, classrooms, committee rooms and a public hall which held 1,200 people for concerts, balls, lectures, flower shows, oratorios and "Saturday night entertainments".

Money from the textile industry funded not only civic architecture on a grand scale but also fabulous houses for the mill owners. One of the finest of these, now open as a museum, is Cliffe Castle in Keighley. Built by Henry Isaac Butterfield, who had made a fortune from worsted trade with the United States, this huge gothic house had marble fountains, conservatories growing bananas and grapes and an estate that stretched from Keighley to Steeton. The textile industry created a well-off middle class who lived in affluent suburbs such as Manningham, Heaton and Higher Spring Gardens, or preferred to commute to Bradford from towns such as Harrogate and Ilkley. The opening of the railway in 1865 connected Ilkley to Otley, Leeds and Bradford and helped to transform the once "dismal village" into an affluent residential town and holiday centre.

As heavy industry has declined there has been a new emphasis on Bradford's landscape and setting. Although the otters observed by Miles Gale have not yet returned, remnants of the landscape which he loved can still be found. Shipley Glen and its ancient woodlands near Saltaire have been a popular beauty spot since Victorian times. In other places such as Goitstock Wood near Cullingworth, nature is busy reclaiming the abandoned mills of the early Industrial Revolution. Two-thirds of Bradford District is still rural, much of it farmland. The moors of grass and heather are criss-crossed by a network of footpaths, including the Pennine Way, which crosses the Worth Valley beyond

Haworth.

Derelict mill,
Bradford.

Stanbury. On a clear day those walking across Oxenhope Moor can see from Emley Moor (south of Dewsbury) to Pen-y-Ghent in the Dales. The top of Baildon Hill offers beautiful vistas across the moors of Ilkley to the north and Haworth to the west, and views across Leeds, Bradford and up the Aire Valley towards Skipton.

The city of Bradford lies in a natural amphitheatre surrounded on three sides by steep hills. The hills can be glimpsed between the façades of the grand Victorian buildings in the city centre. More often, however, tall and ugly concrete buildings which replaced much of old Bradford in the modernisation frenzy of the 1960s and 70s obscure these views. At the end of 2003, ambitious plans were unveiled by the newly formed Urban Regeneration Company to redevelop the city centre. The scheme includes getting rid of the choking inner ring road that reduces much of the city to a series of traffic islands. Many of the newer buildings would be demolished, opening up once more views of the Victorian buildings that survive and of the hills beyond. Water would again play an important role in the city, with the canal being rebuilt and Bradford Beck, which currently runs underground, brought back up to the surface. If this vision becomes reality, the watercourses on which Bradford was built could play an important part in the revival of a great city.

Goitstock on Hewenden Beck near Hallas Bridge.

Drystone walls and barn formerly used for storing food for livestock on the moors above Addingham.

Sources of power, old and new. A steam crane at a quarry in Fagley frames the Bradford Industrial Museum, and a wind turbine is used to power the machinery extracting stone above Haworth. The landscape around Bradford is dotted with stone quarries still in production as well as many disused workings.

From Left to Right:
A historical re-enactment at East Riddlesden Hall near Keighley. This seventeenth century merchant's house, a reminder of the industrial wealth and power of that time, fell into disrepair and was used as a farm before it was restored by The National Trust.

The Manor House in Ilkley was the home of the Middleton family, a long line of lords of the manor who administered local justice from a court held here. Standing on the site of the Roman fort Olicana, the building is now a museum.

View of Bingley from across the River Aire. This ancient settlement, which is mentioned in the Domesday Book, grew up along the banks of the river which would have provided water for washing, cooking and livestock. The Leeds-Liverpool Canal also passes through the town, which meant that many mills were established here, one of the biggest being Damart's mill. Although there is no longer any production at this site it remains the headquarters for Damart's catalogue business.

View of Haworth. One of the early mills of the area can be seen lying derelict at the bottom of the valley.

Housing in the village of Harden. The buildings in the foreground are typical weavers' cottages used by the domestic textile industry before the mills took over.

As the town of Bradford expanded it swallowed many of the hamlets and villages that surrounded it. This farmhouse and school house were originally part of the village of Manningham, remnants of which can still be found clustered around St. Paul's Church. This area is now considered part of inner-city Bradford.

Settlements more remote from areas of urban expansion have retained their own identity, such as Haworth which has kept its cobbled high street and a daily milk round.

Top Left: Keighley Town Hall, part of which was originally the Post Office. By the beginning of the twentieth century Keighley was developing from a ramshackle warren of narrow streets and alleys into a better planned town with spacious streets lined by grand buildings. Impressive banks were built along a widened North Street, and smart shops opened along newly erected Cavendish Street (Bottom Left).

Top Right: The Victorians who built the Town Hall wanted a building that reflected Bradford's status as a metropolis of international standing. The fine result is dominated by a 200-foot clock tower inspired by the bell-tower of the Palazzo Vecchio in Florence.

LANDSCAPE

In the 1850s Titus Salt created not only a mill but also a community to run it. Appalled by the terrible conditions in central Bradford, he had his model village, Saltaire, designed and built several miles to the north on the banks of the River Aire.

At one time the largest factory in the world, the mill complex carried out all the processes necessary to convert raw materials into finished cloth. The workers were provided with housing, together with a school, a hospital, baths, laundry, shops, and a magnificent venue for entertainment, Victoria Hall (Far Left). The deliberate omission was a public house; instead the workers were encouraged to attend the church Salt had built (and where his remains are now entombed). To remind the workforce that it all belonged to the company many of the streets were named after the Salt family. This unique village has now been designated a World Heritage Site.

This page: The European merchant community which came to Bradford in the nineteenth century created the international system of trade that made Bradford the centre of the world's worsted industry. Their legacy to Bradford is Little Germany, a collection of grand warehouses built in the 1860s and 1870s. This area is now home to a variety of service industries including the Bradford Chamber of Commerce which the merchants helped to establish over 150 years ago.

Opposite page, Left to Right:
The Technical School was opened by the then Prince of Wales in 1882 in response to a need for improved design and technical skills for workers in the textile and associated industries. It is now part of Bradford and Ilkley Community College.

Lister's Manningham Mills was the biggest silk and velvet mill in the world. It was built by Samuel Cunliffe Lister, an inventor and businessman, with the fortune he had made from his invention of the wool combing machine. The factory employed 5,000 people at its height, and the Lister's empire included not only the surrounding houses but also such assets as its own collieries in Wales and the railway rolling stock needed to transport the coal to Bradford.

Left: Peel Square is just off Westgate in Bradford city centre, and is a focus of settlement for the Bangladeshi community.

Above: Terraced housing in the Manningham area of Bradford.

Above: View of housing from Keighley town centre. Many terraces of the type seen in the foreground were cleared away in the post-war rebuilding programmes and replaced with houses such as those at the top of the picture.

Many of the houses erected during this period were built as part of large estates that ringed the industrial centres. When the factories closed they left areas of economic hardship. Ravenscliffe estate (Right) is one of those that is now struggling with the effects of mass unemployment and poverty.

Far Right: Some of the industrial buildings in the more desirable areas of the district have escaped demolition and have been converted into homes, such as these former silk mills on the banks of the Leeds-Liverpool Canal in Bingley.

# LANDSCAPE

Opposite page: This viaduct near Cullingworth (Top) is one of the legacies of the extraordinary (and alas now vanished) network of local railways that enabled people to travel around the district.

Two of the great feats of engineering locally are Three Rise Locks (Bottom Left) and Five Rise Locks (Far Left). These lift the Leeds-Liverpool Canal up a steep rise in the Aire valley at Bingley.

Bottom Right: Railways provided a cheaper and faster way of transporting goods than the canals. Bradford became the intersection for several routes, and by 1846 was already connected to Keighley, Bingley, Shipley, Leeds and the national network.

This page: Travel by road is now the dominant mode of transport. Some developments, such as the new bus station in Keighley, have been a success. Others, such as the inner ring road in Bradford, are now considered planning disasters, and have forced pedestrians in many areas of the city, such as Petergate, into a series of subterranean passages.

The skyline of the district is punctuated by a vast array of places of worship of every kind. The Abundant Life Centre (Above) boasts one of the biggest congregations in the country, and its Christmas lights can be seen shining from its elevated position in Wapping overlooking central Bradford. Bradford's biggest mosque (Opposite Page) is being built at the foot of Lumb Lane in the city centre.

View of Bradford Grammar School, Cartwright Hall and Lister's Mill from Bolton Woods. The greenery is Lister Park, which has recently been transformed by a programme combining the renovation of some of its finest Victorian features with the creation of its own Mughal Gardens.

The ruined church in Thornton where the Revd. Patrick Bronte preached before the family moved to nearby Haworth. Between 1816 and 1820 all the famous Bronte daughters, and their brother Branwell, were born in Thornton.

The skills of stone masons are still evident all over the district, decorating everything from humble dwellings to grand mills and warehouses.

The Bradford Cemetery company bought twenty-six acres of land at Undercliffe in 1851 and interred 123,000 people before going into liquidation in the 1970s. The original cemetery was divided up by a land surveyor, Joseph Smith, into areas with a scale of different charges, determined in part by the view from the plots! Wealth determined where you were buried, and the size and splendour of the monument erected in your memory. This view is along the main promenade towards the obelisk commemorating Joseph Smith himself.

View from Wrose across Shipley
and along the Aire Valley.

PEOPLE

# PEOPLE

As with its landscape and buildings, the peopling of Bradford district has been shaped by its industrial past. In 1799 when the first textile mill opened in the small market town of Bradford, the population of Keighley was only 5,000, and Ilkley was described as "an isolated community and dismal village". As more and more mills were built, thousands of people came here to seek work, initially from the surrounding countryside and then from much further afield. By 1850 Bradford had become the fastest-growing town of the Industrial Revolution, home to over 100,000 people; the population of Keighley had more than tripled; and Ilkley was known as an attractive spa town, a desirable neighbourhood for those who had made their money from the nearby factories.

Top: Graveyard, Bingley.

Above: Man in Little Horton.

Right: Sorting historic records at West Yorkshire Archives, based in a converted wool warehouse in central Bradford.

Although the textile industry flourished and huge fortunes were made by the elite who dominated Bradford, this extraordinary economic growth made life appalling for most people. Bradford in the 1840s has been compared to a Wild West town, with widespread lawlessness, crime, violence, drunkenness and prostitution. Living conditions were terrible. The canal basin bubbled with raw sewage in hot weather, and occasionally caught fire. Half of all children died before their fifth birthday and the graveyard around the Parish Church was so full that it disgorged corpses onto Church Bank during landslips. There were frequent cholera epidemics.

Partly because conditions were so squalid, Bradford became the birthplace of social, political and educational reforms. It was the first city to introduce free school milk and school dinners. Free libraries and school baths were opened, educational reform implemented, and medical examinations offered to the public. In 1893 the city made a major contribution to British political life when the Independent Labour Party, forerunner of the Labour Party, was founded in Bradford after a bitter strike at Lister's Mills.

From the Industrial Revolution onwards, immigration has been a distinctive feature of the Bradford district. When Jonathan Glyde arrived in Bradford to become a minister at Horton Lane Congregational Chapel in 1834, he wrote about his new neighbours: "the natives of Scotland are here, the natives of Ireland are here, from the pleasant vales of Devonshire men and women have come: from the banks of the Rhine and the Elbe they are coming". Many people arrived from central and western Ireland, and by 1851 the Irish made up ten percent of the population of Bradford and five percent of Keighley. From the other end of the class spectrum, wealthy European merchants came to Bradford to be on the spot where cloth was produced and then to sell it throughout the world.

The cultural mix of Bradford changed little from the late nineteenth century to the end of the Second World War. The post-war boom attracted workers from central and eastern Europe, often people who had been displaced by the War. In the 1950s and 60s the mills and foundries introduced new working practices including night shifts just as better-paid jobs in other sectors became available.

The result was a labour shortage in the mills and workers were recruited from overseas, particularly men from India, Pakistan and Bangladesh. People also came in smaller numbers from many of the West Indian islands to work in public transport and the health service. As the new Immigration Acts of the early 1960s made it more difficult for Asian men to come and go between Britain and their homelands, many decided to stay and sent for their families to join them. More recent arrivals include refugees from East Africa, Vietnam, and Bosnia.

This steady history of incomers and 'offcumdens' has given Bradford a quality noted by JB Priestley, who recalled growing up in a city that was "one of the most provincial and yet one of the most cosmopolitan of English cities... There was this odd mixture in pre-[First World]War Bradford. A dash of the Rhine and the Oder found its way into our grim runnel - 't' mucky beck'. Bradford was determinedly Yorkshire and provincial, yet some of its suburbs reached as far as Frankfurt or Leipzig".

Today those connections stretch much further, to cities such as Warsaw and Lviv, to the islands of Dominica and Barbados, and as far as rural areas in northern Pakistan and Bangladesh. The urban centres of Bradford and Keighley have become classic examples of complex multicultural societies, surrounded by towns, villages and rural areas where the same families have lived for hundreds of years.

Above: Before the construction of turnpikes, or toll roads, in the 1700s, packhorses were the main mode of transport in the area. Trains of horses carried goods along narrow flagged footpaths and bridle tracks, crossing streams on narrow bridges such as this one over Harden Beck near Bingley.

Left: Some of the earliest evidence of people living in the area dates from the Bronze Age (1500 to 500 BC) and includes the many carved rocks scattered over Rombalds Moor, such as the Swastika Stone above Ilkley.

Gravestone in Haworth churchyard. In the mid-1800s tuberculosis was the main cause of death. Congested slums, overflowing privies, open cesspits, pigsties, slaughterhouses and contaminated water supplies all contributed to the spread of disease. Cholera epidemics were common and the newly-established Local Board of Health reported typhus fever as being "very bad" in Stanbury and Oxenhope.

In Memory of
MERCY,
Daughter of Abraham & Matty Sunderland
of Stanbury, who died July 11th 1864.

Wedding at St. Patrick's Church in Westgate, Bradford. The settlement of the Irish communities in nineteenth century Bradford and Keighley is reflected today in the location of the surviving Roman Catholic churches, St. Mary's, St. Patrick's, St. Anne's and St. Joseph's. As with so many other migrant groups these places of worship acted as crucial centres of support and solidarity. The priests and nuns acted not only as spiritual mentors but also performed many other vital roles for their often Gaelic-speaking congregations, who were treated with deep hostility by locals because they were Roman Catholics.

Lighting the gas lamps at The New Beehive Inn. Adjacent to St. Patrick's Church and built in 1902, it replaced the original Beehive Inn, a popular Irish pub established in the mid-1800s.

The Reform Jewish Synagogue in Bowland Street, Manningham. Many of the European merchants who came to Bradford in the early 1800s were Jewish. Consecrated in 1881, the synagogue is now rarely used as the nearest active Jewish communities are now in Leeds and Manchester.

Tony Lidington, Fellow in Theatre at Bradford University, explores a derelict weaving shed at Lister's Mill in Manningham. He was writing *Velvet and Brass*, a musical that commemorated the centenary of the 1891 strike at Bradford's biggest mill. Although the five-month strike ended in a bitter defeat for the workers, it acted as the catalyst for a new alliance between trade unionists and local socialists which led to the founding in Bradford of the Independent Labour Party in 1893, the forerunner of the modern day Labour Party.

This small enclave of houses for retired tradespeople is hidden away in the Manningham area. The carved alpaca goats are a reference to Sir Titus Salt, who sat on the committee which founded the houses. Wool from the alpaca goat was the basis of Salt's textile fortune and was woven at his mill in Saltaire.

A woman with her cat in Denholme, and another (Right) sweeping the street outside her home in Stanbury. These villages, like many others in the area, grew up as agricultural settlements whose inhabitants earned extra money from textile manufacture. Stanbury and Denholme were also places where coal was mined, which became particularly important with the advent of steam power.

The Queensbury Support Centre running a luncheon club in the local Baptist Church. Queensbury was originally a tiny hilltop hamlet, which grew into a large community to service the huge Black Dyke Mills. The owner of the mill, John Foster, provided a number of amenities for the village including the library, the swimming baths, and the gas supply.

Opposite page:
In the late 1940s many people displaced from their homelands by the Second World War settled in Bradford. The Poles were the largest such group, unwilling to return to a country ruled by a Communist regime controlled by Stalin's Russia. This woman is holding the only two things her Polish mother brought with her to Britain: her Polish bible, and a photograph of her with the bible on the farm in Germany where she was forced to work during the War.

Top Left:
A number of groups came from countries occupied by Russia at the end of the War. Together they formed Captive Nations, a group which campaigned for the rights of their countries to independence from Soviet control. In the 1990s their hopes were finally fulfilled with the collapse of the Soviet Union.

Top Right:
An Italian family getting ready for the wedding of their daughter at St. Walburga's Church in Shipley. The Italian community became firmly established here with the recruitment of women to work in the textile mills in the late 1940s and 50s.

Bottom Right:
Easter service held at the Serbian Orthodox Church in Little Horton.

Bottom Left:
During the service at the Serbian Orthodox Church candles are lit for the health of the living and in memory of the dead.

Man at prayer in the Ukrainian Orthodox Church, a converted Wesleyan Chapel in Eccleshill. Bradford's Ukrainian community is the largest in western Europe, and although most originate from Western Ukraine and are members of the Ukrainian Catholic Church, there are significant numbers of people from Eastern Ukraine who adhere to the Orthodox faith.

Remembering the dead at Nab Wood Cemetery in Shipley.

After Ukraine's independence from the Soviet Union in 1991, Ukrainians were able to travel freely in and out of their country. The visit of the Ukrainian National Folk Ensemble to a packed Alhambra Theatre as part of the 1991 Bradford Festival was a very emotional occasion.

Left: A Saturday school at the Association of Ukrainians in Great Horton. Children go on Saturdays to learn the language, history and culture of Ukraine. For fifty years Ukraine was part of the Soviet Union, and the Ukrainian language, religions and customs were banned by the Communist regime.

# PEOPLE

From Left to Right:
A photograph taken during the 1950s at The Belle Vue Studio in Manningham on display at Bradford Industrial Museum. This portrait studio was popular with families newly-arrived from the West Indies who often wanted pictures to send back to family and friends in the Caribbean.

Playing dominoes outside the Dominican Association in Westgate. Roughly two-thirds of the Afro-Caribbean community in Bradford originate from Dominica, and the rest from Jamaica, Barbados, and the Leeward and Windward Islands.

Celebrating the South Bradford carnival with a procession through the streets of West Bowling, where many of the Afro-Caribbean community live.

Calling to friends from the window of a beauty parlour.

In the early 1960s changes in the immigration laws made it much harder for migrant workers to come and go, and jobs were becoming harder to obtain. As a result many men sent for their wives and children to join them in England, and a transient workforce became a settled community. Many of the women found employment in areas traditionally reserved for females, such as spinning silk at Bingley Mills, or making up curtains at Manningham Mills.

The Asian community first established itself in the area when men came to work in the textile and engineering industries. Most intended to stay a few years, work hard and save money, in order to return to an improved standard of living in their own country. They lived cheaply in shared accommodation close to their work.

The pictures on the opposite page show the Sweet Centre on Lumb Lane (one of the early cafes where the men would gather to eat and socialise), warp preparation at Drummond's Mill, foundry work in Keighley and a pin up in a spinning mill.

Young people take a trip on the Leeds-Liverpool canal.

Far Left: Burning an effigy of Ravana to celebrate the victory of good over evil during the Hindu festival of Navaratri in Great Horton, where many of the Indian Hindu community live. Different parts of Bradford and Keighley have become home to communities from different parts of the Asian sub-continent.

Left: When the Asian communities became established they set up their own places of worship and other organisations. This boy is learning the Koran at one of the many madrassas, or supplementary schools, attached to mosques in the area.

The mosque on Carlisle Road in Manningham is reflected in the window of a local takeaway.

Mohammed Ajeeb is embraced by his father during his inauguration as Lord Mayor at Bradford City Hall in 1985. He was Britain's first Asian Lord Mayor.

**The future of Bradford...**
the district's children and young people attend 208 state schools, as well as numerous private day schools and nurseries.

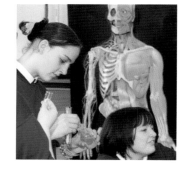

PEOPLE

00

All sorts of different wedding ceremonies take place locally.

Clockwise from above:
The night before a Hindu wedding women gather to sing songs; a white wedding at Bingley Parish Church; and a Muslim groom arrives for his wedding party at the Carlisle Business Centre where he will be given brightly coloured sweets.

The Queen visited Bradford Cathedral in 1997 for the Maundy Thursday service, led by the Bishop of Bradford and remembering the last acts of Jesus's life. She also went to Centenary Square where she met the assembled crowds and laid a wreath at the monument commemorating the fire at Valley Parade football ground in which 56 people lost their lives.

Saturday afternoon crowd in Centenary Square gathered for a Bradford Festival event.

LEISURE

# LEISURE

The Woolpack in Esholt, the area's best-known pub, which features in the TV soap *Emmerdale*.

'A Surprising Place' was the cheeky phrase Bradford used to promote itself in the early 1980s, and despite the scepticism of many local inhabitants, it seemed to work. People's preconceptions of Bradford as a grimy city full of dark satanic mills began to fall away. Virtually all the chimneys have gone now, and although some stereotypes seem harder to shake off, eight million visitors now come to the Bradford district each year, drawn by the richness of its landscape and architecture and the diversity of its attractions.

Windsurfing in the Worth Valley and playground at Sandy Lane, near Wilsden.

Alternative fashion show at the Midland Hotel.

The most prominent of these is the National Museum of Photography, Film and Television, the most visited museum in the UK outside London. Its spectacular glass façade overlooks Bradford city centre, housing five floors of interactive galleries and exhibitions and three cinemas including the massive IMAX screen. The museum hosts three film festivals annually: the Bradford Film Festival, Bite the Mango Black and Asian Film Festival, and BAF! - Bradford Animation Festival.

Next door is the Alhambra Theatre with its distinctive Moorish architecture. This theatre pulls in crowds from all across the North with its lavish Christmas pantomimes, and hosts an extensive programme of national and international touring shows. Other performance venues in the centre of Bradford include St George's Concert Hall, Bradford University's Theatre in the Mill, and the Priestley Centre for the Arts. Across the district venues such as Ilkley Playhouse, Bingley Arts Centre, Keighley Playhouse and Keighley's Victoria Hall provide a space for performances by professional and amateur groups. Home-grown musical talent includes many popular groups with a national profile, ranging from teen idol Gareth Gates, heavy metal band Terrorvision, to the Black Dyke Mills Band and the Steeton Male Voice Choir.

There is a rich variety of festivals to be enjoyed. Each year the Ilkley Literature Festival attracts an impressive list of household names to the north of England's premier literary event. For many years Bradford has promoted its summer festival as the biggest celebration of community-led arts in the country, mixing international acts with aspiring and established local talent. The Lord Mayor's Carnival Parade and the Bradford Mela are the festival's showpiece events, both riotous blends of noise and colour that celebrate the diverse heritage of Bradford's communities. Other community-led events see carnival queens crowned and hundreds of cups and prizes awarded at fairs, shows and galas held throughout the summer in the district's rural towns and villages.

For those interested in the visual arts, Cartwright Hall - bequeathed to the people of Bradford by textile magnate Samuel Lister - is home to extensive collections of British and South Asian art, together with an exciting programme of temporary exhibitions. Samuel Lister's great rival Titus Salt built his mill a few miles north of Bradford in Saltaire, and it now houses a huge collection of work by Bradford-born artist David Hockney. Meanwhile in Keighley Cliffe Castle Museum is the former home of another Victorian textile giant, Henry Isaac Butterfield. Parts of this museum preserve the opulent grandeur in which the Butterfield family lived, and the rest reflects the social, natural and

Sunday football at Harden.

A fourteen-year-old dancer from Java in an international festival of theatre outside St George's Hall.

Taking flight from Baildon Hill.

industrial history of the area. Bradford's industrial history can also be explored at Moorside Mills, a former spinning mill in the Eccleshill area of the city. Three of the oldest buildings in the area are open to the public - seventeenth-century East Riddlesden Hall and Bolling Hall, and the fourteenth-century Manor House Museum in Ilkley.

As well as these 'flagship' buildings there are many leisure centres offering activities like ice-skating and bowling, over 400 pubs, nightclubs and small music venues, and 200 hotels. There are more than 150 gyms and fitness centres, over 100 amateur soccer clubs, and the amateur cricket leagues are arguably the best in the country. There are also three professional sports teams: the hugely successful Rugby League team Bradford Bulls, the Keighley Cougars rugby team, and Bradford City Football Club. Bradford's best-kept secret is undoubtedly its scenery. Two-thirds of the area is countryside, beautiful wooded valleys alternating with high heather moorland, all of it easily accessible to visitors. The Worth Valley steam railway takes day trippers from Keighley into the heart of the landscape made famous by its connection with the Bronte sisters. Standing on the moors above Haworth or by the ancient cup-and-ring carved stones on Ilkley Moor, it's easy to see why Bradford remains a surprising place, both for visitors and residents alike.

The Bradford Bulls on their way to victory against their neighbours and Rugby League rivals Leeds Rhinos at their home ground, Odsal Stadium. In a long list of great achievements, their finest moment came in February 2002 when they beat the Australian team Newcastle Knights to claim the title of World Club Champions.

Fans at Valley Parade experiencing the ups and downs of supporting Bradford City Football Club as they suffer a defeat against Portsmouth in the Nationwide First Division.

Shipley Providence Cricket Club playing a Sunday League match on the banks of the River Aire.

Cricket is a hugely popular pastime played in the streets and back alleys of Bradford.

Filling a steam engine with water at Keighley station. The Keighley and Worth Valley Railway is a fully-restored branch line that runs regular services between Keighley and Oxenhope. Maintained and staffed by a team of volunteers, the line is a popular location for feature films, such as The Railway Children, Yanks, and Harry Potter.

CLASS 78

3rd

Prizewinners on display at the
Methodist Church in Baildon.

1st prize

Admiring the size of a pumpkin at the Baildon
Horticultural Society's 52nd Annual Flower,
Vegetable and Handicraft Show.

Young gardener,
Baildon Green.

Late summer display,
Esholt.

Methodist Church,
Baildon.

Founded in 1983, the National Museum of Photography, Film & Television attracts approximately 750,000 visitors each year. Its collection contains more than three million items, including the original cameras used to create the Cottingley Fairy photographs, one of the most notorious photographic hoaxes of all time.

A part of the National Museum of Science and Industry, the decision to locate the Museum in Bradford was driven by the city's historic contribution to the development of cinema and film-making in the UK. Tom Courtney is pictured here at the launch of Bradford's film heritage trail, returning to the city where he starred in the 1960s classic *Billy Liar*, and *The Dresser,* which was filmed at the Alhambra Theatre.

115

Right: Cartwright Hall Art Gallery was opened in 1904 in the shadow of Lister's Manningham Mills. It was built with funds donated by Samuel Lister on the site of his former home, the grounds of which now form Lister Park.

Far Right: Artist Bhajan Hunjan preparing a dance floor for performances linked to her exhibition at Cartwright Hall.

Below: Children and staff from Frizinghall Primary School working with the Cartwright Hall collections on National Children's Art Day.

Above: Cliffe Castle Museum in Keighley was built as a millionaire's mansion between 1875 and 1882, financed by proceeds from the local textile industry. It opened as a museum in 1959 and is set in an attractive park.

Visitors examine some of the hundreds of works by David Hockney permanently on display at Salts Mill. Both Hockney and the man who bought and renovated Salts Mill, Jonathan Silver, were pupils at Bradford Grammar School. Arguably the world's most famous living artist, Hockney started his career at Bradford College of Art.

Line dancing club.

Tea dance.

Members of Concert Brass, one of the three brass bands sponsored by Yorkshire Building Society since 1993. Yorkshire Building Society Brass Band are the current European Champions, a title they have held for seven out of the last eight years. They are also the current British Open Champions.

Trumpeter in Femi Kuti's *Afrobeats* who performed in Centenary Square, Bradford, as part of a nationwide celebration of music, BBC Music Live.

Dancing to a jazz band in Myrtle Park, Bingley, which hosts a regular programme of music and other outdoor events.

Bradford has been the birthplace for many hugely popular bands (from left to right) experienced troupers New Model Army and Smokie, to new boy at the top of the charts, Gareth Gates.

LEISURE

Breakdancing at a club night held in Bradford's West End, a popular destination for young people on a night out.

A member of the locally-based street band The Peace Artistes plays from a float built by Ali Allen and Marise Rose as part of Bradford Festival, an annual summer celebration held all over the city.

Dancing to the rumba played by Sam Mangwana from Zaire.

During the Festival's varied programme of street performance Maynard Flip Flap, a man who appears to live in a box, is greeted by a shopper.

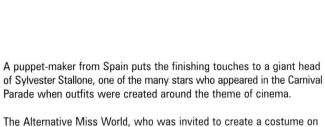

A puppet-maker from Spain puts the finishing touches to a giant head of Sylvester Stallone, one of the many stars who appeared in the Carnival Parade when outfits were created around the theme of cinema.

The Alternative Miss World, who was invited to create a costume on the theme of Bradford.

The annual Carnival Parade is led each year by the Lord Mayor, seen here waving from his howdah. When she is not travelling to events across the country Lulu the Elephant can be seen on the roof of the Aagrah Restaurant in Shipley.

A rugby club member takes a break during the Parade.

The Bradford Festival Mela attracts over 100,000 people to Peel Park over a summer weekend to enjoy a multi-cultural programme of arts, sports, music, food and performance with an Asian flavour. Mela was originally a Sanskrit word meaning gathering, and the Bradford Mela is the largest such event outside the Asian subcontinent.

The Alhambra Theatre has hosted everything from internationally acclaimed dance companies such as Alvin Ailey (top left) and Nederlans Dance Theatre (above) to youth workshops run by the National Association for Indian Dance (top right). The production of *Gormenghast* (bottom right) by David Glass premiered here with a show that helped establish Glass's company as top flight performers of physical theatre.

As well as its famous pantomimes Bradford is the source of many shows by amateur and professional companies each year. Clockwise from top left: *Robinson Crusoe* starring David Essex at the Alhambra Theatre. Red Ladder Theatre Company's *Low Down High Notes* at Theatre in the Mill charted the search by a teenager for singing stardom. Interviewing residents of Thorpe Edge during the writing of *A State Affair*, Out of Joint Theatre's devastating account of the effects of poverty and hard drugs on Bradford's housing estates. *Streets of Rage* by the Asian Theatre School explored the reaction of local residents to the riots of 2001.

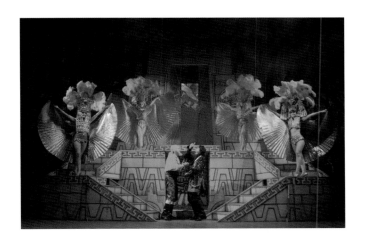

Although water courses were fundamentally important to the growth of towns and industries in the area, they are now more likely to be used for recreation, such as fishing in the River Aire at Saltaire or paddling in the River Wharfe at Ilkley.

Riding across the moors at Swartha, near Silsden.

Setting off for a winter walk on the
St Ives Estate at Harden.